The Air is Elastic

The Air is Elastic

Ella Zeltserman

TURNSTONE PRESS

The Air Is Elastic
copyright © Ella Zeltserman 2018

Turnstone Press
Artspace Building
206-100 Arthur Street
Winnipeg, MB
R3B 1H3 Canada
www.TurnstonePress.com

All rights reserved. No part of this book may be reproduced or transmitted in any form or by any means—graphic, electronic or mechanical—without the prior written permission of the publisher. Any request to photocopy any part of this book shall be directed in writing to Access Copyright, Toronto.

Turnstone Press gratefully acknowledges the assistance of the Canada Council for the Arts, the Manitoba Arts Council, the Government of Canada, and the Province of Manitoba through the Book Publishing Tax Credit and the Book Publisher Marketing Assistance Program.

Cover photograph: GOLD FOLIAGE Hand Dyed Silk Scarf by Silk Scarves Colorado, www.etsy.com/shop/silkscarvescolorado.

Printed and bound in Canada.

Library and Archives Canada Cataloguing in Publication

Zeltserman, Ella, 1955-, author
    The air is elastic / Ella Zeltserman.

Poems.
Issued in print and electronic formats.
ISBN 978-0-88801-633-1 (softcover).--ISBN 978-0-88801-634-8 (EPUB).--
ISBN 978-0-88801-635-5 (Kindle).--ISBN 978-0-88801-636-2 (PDF)

    I. Title.

PS8649.E52A75 2018   C811'.6   C2018-901370-2
    C2018-901371-0

for Mark, with love

Contents

Private Details of Our Lives

Private Details of Our Lives / 7
Smouldering Core / 8
Pietà / 9
Spring / 10
Drop by Drop / 11
Variations on Twilight / 12
Blind / 24
Waiting for You / 25
Fluctuations / 26
Chalat / 28
We Expected Sedona to Be Red and Warm / 29
I Do Not Know Where *There* Is / 30
At the Door / 31
God Came down for Beauty / 32
Sunday Morning Breakfast / 34
Solaris / 36
Reading Brodsky / 37
Somebody Mourned James Dean / 38
Melting Winter Afternoon / 40
Air / 41
That Last Leaf / 42

A Vast Sea

A Vast Sea / 45
Tselina / 55

Visit to an Ancestral Village / 56
Upon Waking / 58
Continental Divide / 59
Morning Sigh / 60
Black Snow / 61
Bursting / 62
Do You Remember Our Life? / 76
On His Breath / 78
Night Vigil / 81
In the Family Room / 82
Sea Waves / 84
Roman Bus / 86
Two Knit, Two Purl / 87
Double-Edged / 88
Rupture / 89
Almost a Recipe / 90
Queen of the Neva / 92
Volodia / 94
That One Small Step / 96

As We Trot the Surface of the Globe

Almodrote / 99
White Petals / 112

Notes on the Poems / 123
Acknowledgements / 127

The Air is Elastic

toskà—*the inexplicable, indefinite feeling that hints at unappeasable heartache, an insatiable longing to reach out beyond accessible reality*

Private Details of Our Lives

Private Details of Our Lives

Can you see my heart hidden in a jar of jam?
Can you touch the moonlight I baked
into the cake? Can you smell our night of love

in the chocolate raspberry tart? The pulse of my life
on the tip of a whisk. I watch a hot bead slide
from a spoon onto my nail. Eye the glistening globule

like my mother did. Years of experience to judge
it right. The drop from my heart sets tight. Jam
is ready. My love in a jar. I turn the bowl

of whipped egg whites upside down. They do not slide.
Ready, Aunt Ida would say. I offer you a taste of sunshine,
light summery day, happiness on your fork

with the milky-warm scent of vanilla. I teach my daughter
a little trick I use. Cook your beets in something sour. Magic
to turn earth's roots into gleaming, red rubies.

Smouldering Core

You look into my eyes, hold me,
shelter me from the world outside and ask,
what are you afraid of?
I listen inside and answer—*life*.

I hear the turning earth screech.
I feel the tremors
of her breathing volcanoes,
her magma heat under my feet.
I see the clouds gathering into storms,
understand birds' anxious cries, frantic flight.

I smell the utter sadness of melting snow,
touch the air of morning
crammed with shadows of the night,
taste the blood of your lips in the dark.

I am the hurried kisses
between night and dawn in the seconds
they part from each other,
that last song of love falling leaves sing
to a spent land in autumn,
the tiredness of a disillusioned sun at sunset,
the stillness of noon,
the despair of twilight.

Pietà

Last time I saw you, all was quiet in St. Peter's.
You sat in the cathedral's niche for several hundred years.
People peacefully walked around, stopped to say hello

or confide in you. Do you remember me? I had my baby
in a stroller, you held your dead son on your
knees, and we talked mother to mother. I heard

the mute grief in your eyes, your listless hands told
of end. The folds of your dress fell down like a body
to earth. The irrevocability of death, the silence. Your anguish

so shattering in its calmness, beyond human endurance. You bowed
to the will of God. I cried. You could not anymore. We were both
so young. You still are. Do you remember? I came now to say,

I understand you much more. I bring my adult daughter
to meet you. But you cannot hear us. A glass wall surrounds you,
your nose is cracked, crowds push around. You are an attraction,

a sculpted animal in the zoo. Most stop for a moment to record
they've been here, gawking at a mother's unbroken sorrow.
Barrage of flashing cameras—a submachine gun directed at you.

Spring

Waxwings get drunk on mountain ash berries
fermented by tedious winter into a bird's Cabernet
Franc. Soft-grey passerines dive, kamikaze style,

straight into the windows that wrap our house
in a miracle of sunlight. We hide, perched inside,
listen to crashing knocks on the glass, talk about

Hitchcock's bird attacks. Warm spring sun sets,
ends the drink-and-fly revelry. We get out, pick up
the small, fluffy bodies. Black throats to bury.

Drop by Drop

Standing in the shower I think
how eco-unfriendly I am,
pouring so much hot water
on my short frame. How the drops
land on the glass door, none
ever reaching the floor in a nascent
shape. Each little drop loses
itself, merging into one wall
of water. How that quivering wall
on my door hides the world
outside and I stay in the middle
of man made rain   separated.

Variations on Twilight

1
my twilight starts at sunset
as the day drops into night
symerky permeates my world

2
I like a bright day or a dark night
twilight brings despair

debilitates
as I watch

my shadow
growing darker and darker

merging into night
disappearing

as the day sinks
leaving me unarmed

3
people saunter
chat, smile

no fear
of passing moments
fading day
nearing the end

4
an inexplicable
time between day and night
something not quite
something you cannot touch

sun goes down
day ends
gives night a chance
to beckon her shadows into vanishing light

5
a longing
for something departing
something you still can see
as it expires, diffuses into thin air

like two people together for a few more moments
parting
unable to change the course of their destiny
grey strokes on a mercury sky

6
aura of parting
in the morning
the leftover stew for one

acrid odour
night extinguishes the flame
does not turn off the gas burner

7
I am like a bird
at the coming of a storm

cannot explain
how she knows
what in the air
what tells her to flee
fly down toward the earth

the wings of my heart flap
frantic
at the inevitable

8
I do not smile
my heart either beats too fast
or slows down to a murmur

my eyes cast down
I mourn the day
frightened by night's shadows

I hear time stir
creak
as the clock moves

a notch
a notch
a notch

9
sad grey
subdues carmine
tints the purple

disguises the sharpness
of day's end
the catastrophe

10
as the day sinks
I hide inside
blinds drawn
eyes heavy

night comes
my rescue
blankets bleak
with black

11
mini hurricane
vortex

colliding day and night
on their way in and out
of our lives

shatters the shaky divide
between day
and the nocturnal spectre of the past

rises
unstoppable miasma

fetid vapour of centuries
crawling inside
a void left by the waning

12
day dissolves into night
last breath
dies

night mourns
ebony
grief so strong she will expire

by the time sun births a new day
without any knowledge
of this night

Blind

Please, pull the blinds down
                        one by one.
Twilight can seep through glass
                        and I am naked
                        opened by your love
                        I am without armor.

                        Anybody can come in
                        and touch

                        you

                                  time

                                          God

                                                  twilight.

The room is full of presence from years gone by.
Shadows rise from the dust
and voices from the carpet.

Pull faster, faster
turn on the light
and look into my eyes.

Waiting for You

Phone call. Small talk. Questions about your health
and the weather, about simple actions like taking Allegra
and sleeping. Nothing about your voice that I miss at night
nothing about your hands that I dream of in our bed
that I call mine during these days apart. Our house I call
mine. The rooms empty. The couch bereft without
your drooping head as you fall asleep in its corner
while I read you some Brodsky. My eyes glide
unobstructed from chair to chair in a smooth, slow
movement. The garden is lonely. You do not come
in early morning for the daily inspection. I do not tell
you that I am like the garden, and as thirsty. Without
your eyes flowers dare not look so fresh and full-blown.
I hide, wait for the sounds of your feet on the stairs
for your cough in the morning and a quiet good night.
I miss your body, the movements of your hands
as you touch a mug of tea, a fork, a spoon, me. All objects
weightless in a space where you are the magnet.

Without you, things drop, senseless.

Fluctuations

today my smile freezes
your touch does not reach
last night our furnace hiccupped
the temperature wobbles, down, then up

unstable connection you say
cold in your eyes
no spark in mine
down and up, up and down

we watch
a Roman history on DVD
monotony of killings
swords thrust, heads cut

we sit
you say Ecclesiastes
I say bad director
the furnace holds up, it's warmer

~

in bed I toss
the whole day in my head
it is all so old
so long ago

queen Cartimandua collaborated
Caratacus did not
Germanicus died
Arminius killed

I toss, all is past
Rome, my sad heart
ecclesiast, the battles inside
the night

Chalat

I am mellowing into you
into your old, frayed *chalat*
into the way you eat without a plate
into your sleep, into your smile

I am mellowing into you
along the veins on your legs
on the surface of your scratched skin
into your time-spotted hands

I am mellowing into you
on your grey, balding head
fading in your once-bright eyes
now unrecognizable in old photographs

I am mellowing into you
ripening
cell by cell
into dust

We Expected Sedona to Be Red and Warm

no sky, no mountain, no ground
for a backdrop—thick white nothingness
on it—a scrawny pine tree
green-grey junipers
snowflakes fall—white on white
in bed—hand in hand—we abide
silence
envelops us
the room, the window
merges
with the nothingness

if I removed my hand
from under the blanket
stretched fingers
I would touch
time's drift
as it moves through the room
as it seeps through walls
into whiteness
and my life and my love
with it
into an impregnable nothing

I Do Not Know Where *There* Is

the gust of wind
the scent of spring
the long-ago kiss on cheek

and slightly opened door
and light through curtains
and heat of bodies touched by love

there, there   in the distance
we can no longer reach
nor travel to such tenderness

hearts get coarse
from northern winds
we do not bend, we persevere

winds win in subtle ways
by chilling voice
by drying lips

the days become much the same
the change is measured
in the grey

in wrinkles on the face
in cracks in smiles
morning after morning

At the Door

Sun comes up every morning
night follows day
wind—I cannot direct
time—I cannot smell
touch, or stop its march.

I wait for you
the door opens.
An unknown grey-haired man walks in
a question in his eyes.
Who is this woman in my house?

We kiss.

God Came down for Beauty

I made peace with my life. I made
peace with the world. I spent years
shaking my fists at God.

So much anger   so much pain
so much fighting for every day
as I dragged my fatigued limbs

across the fractured tempest of my life.
Had I written then   my words
would have shaken the heavens   dragged

God down. Instead   I ate myself   daily
at breakfast   dinner   and lunch.
I snacked on my tears   not wiped

by angels. I was almost gone by the time
I surrendered. The words unfurled
night-blooming cereus.

Beauty came forth   not pain
love   not anger   floods of memories
rivers of the past with people on boats

waving at me. We now can recognize
one another. Some already crossed the dark
leaden Styx waiting for me on the other side.

I am not in a rush.
Turns out God loves beauty.
God too wants to smile.

Sunday Morning Breakfast

I whisper into your ear, so you hear,
and do not hear, how I am a Gypsy,
black hair, golden hoops in my ears,
noisy *tabor*, husky voice, songs,
guitars. Stars from the sky meet stars
from the fire. Your eyes—dark of night,
scarlet of flame, pierce my body. I dance,
shake half-naked breasts, faster, faster,
coming closer to you, closer, closer and
your hands, hot and large on my breast,
embrace all of me and you bite.

Whisper how I am a slave in your harem,
bright blue tiles with red tulips, water fountain,
brazier, garnet hot coals warm the room,
my veils quiver. Golden *shalvar*, among
rose petals I lay on the floor at your feet,
tanbur sounds, you smile, almond eyes
burn my limbs, your hands touch
my bare-skinned stomach, I am aflame,
I am blazing.

Hear how I am seated in a camp on the steppes,
wrapped in furs, crimson and gold,
leather boots on my feet. Snow falls,
horses gallop, you snatch me, throw my
lithe and yielding body over your
worn-out saddle, and we laugh as we ride
into the starry night. Nobody can catch us.
Your strong hands at my waist hold me
tight, very tight, and I whisper into your ear,

open eyes, empty pillow, then I hear
dishes clink, your soft steps on the stairs,
coming closer, closer. Your hands carry
a large gilded tray. Blue and white
cups with tea, toast glistens
with red-raspberry jam. You serve me
Sunday breakfast in bed.

Solaris
For Warren W.

What is the ocean in Tarkovsky's *Solaris*?
Grey mercury of quivering shapeless
memory mass, everything and nothing
in its relation to the moments of life.

Depth of despair of human existence
catching us unaware at night.
Life as we want it, without loss
love of perfect dimension and touch.

Ocean of consciousness set to pick up
the tortured souls, the broken hearts
the inner ego, not seen in a daily mirror
the horror, relieved by killing oneself.

Rings of road, one above the other
screeching sound of future cars
a road like a dream's endless cycles
the blast into space, the only wake-up.

For a generation raised without the culture of cars
daily existence is not measured in miles
life from a moving sedan is less real
than from a spaceship suspended in the ocean of time.

Reading Brodsky

We like awards, you got Nobel,
shuffling a deck of cards, best on top
for the moment, gives you the name,

something to refer to, if one can't understand
why, what matters, if words by themselves
are not enough; frozen rivers jet from under

a bridge like *rukav*; dunes, doors, old houses,
chicken cartilage; a bed in a frozen village,
one hundred and one marshy islands; a city like vodka,

petrified into nightmare, colour left there, smell
drifts into now; life—an exile, why
Collected and Nobel? as if pain

can be labelled, as if love can be caught,
fed like a bird, crumbs from the table of the tyrant
who is in the loge, while you in the parterre,

teeth crush the words, spit them; free,
trot the world, Istanbul, Paris, Rome,
talk to God, as equal, *lean over*, you whisper,

gratitude, into the darkness, along Venice canals,
like star in sky, like black ink on paper,
each comma—*toskà*.

Somebody Mourned James Dean

Somebody mourned James Dean
mother? a sister? a friend?
Somebody looked at the empty chair
at breakfast and really mourned.

A generation cried over the loss
of their icon, saddened to this day
their hair greyed, eyes faded
but somebody really mourned

the son, the brother
not this photograph on the wall
of the fifties-themed breakfast room
in a hotel, next to Marilyn's dress

flying into the golden forever.
Somebody mourned James Dean
his eyes staring at the stale coffee
in the half empty cup, his hands

reaching for a knife, spreading butter
on burned toast. Somebody missed
the odour of his sweaty armpits
at night, the smile, the softness

of bare feet on carpet, the yawning
the coughing, the future shuffle.
Somebody folded his shirt and jeans
put away a sweater, the plastic comb

carried the worn-out shoes
to charity, returned, listened to the silence
had a drink, then another, and lived on.
Somebody mourned James Dean.

Melting Winter Afternoon

a line of poetry
the row of knitting
tea in a porcelain cup

outside snow saddens
plunging from its fluffy highs

line of poetry's frosty edges
sparkle of letters
as they glide

birds on the weeping branches
spooked by the errant word

row of knitting
the needles clicking
chatting the lightness of silky wool

gossamer shawl grows
cloud of warmth against expected chill

waft of steam rises
fogs the window into the melting white
the trembles of a hot golden liquid

the heart of the afternoon
in a blue and white cup

Air

I did not understand life, not as a girl
catching bumblebees by their wings,
skipping a rope, two little braids jumping behind.
The air was cotton,
crisp and fresh
like my just-laundered new dress.

Not as young woman finding your love,
soaring to paradise, wings on my back,
I thought life would be bliss.
The air was velvet,
soft and magical
like white clouds covering us every night.

Not as a mother too busy to think
unnecessary things, tending to tempers
and colds, cooking dinner and wiping tears.
That air was elastic,
stretched to the limit
like my weary, overwrought nerves.

Tending the flowers in my garden now,
I watch each day draw to its end,
yellow leaves, the coming of fall.
The air is a shroud,
pungent decay,
rotting leaves crushed under my feet.

That Last Leaf

That last leaf on my cherry tree
bloodless green, lacks
chlorophyll, hidden from light
by the lush life of others
finally shows its anorexic ribs
to the barren sun.

Frost lurks below.

A Vast Sea

A Vast Sea

*Three hundred days I look at the sea,
search for a sign of my lost caravel.*

*We all have our own caravel of hopes.
Don't miss her coming, don't lose.*
—From *Caravel*, an old Soviet song.

I.
Rag in my hands I wash the sink
and ponder how life turns
into such ordinary things—floors, dishes, bathtubs,
rags, towels, cooking dinner, feeding kids.

Seaports, train stations, runways, and beds—
the points where people part, splinter
and leave their spirits to linger over old haunts
like spooky ghosts, like taboo shadows at night.

My ship had sailed. I always thought it was a caravel,
I loved the song,
I was not Columbus or Magellan,
I had small dreams.

Once I saw Scarlet Sails floating on the Neva
along the granite embankments of St. Petersburg,
one day a year at White Nights,
a romantic gesture in the grim reality of Soviet lives.

That voyage finished in predictable realms.

My caravel went farther,
I steered into unknown seas, looked for monsters in the deep.
The hourly broadcasts of ancient mariners were lies—
there was no abyss, no edge to fall over, I docked on the other side.

II.
Cold Baltic water runs through my blood.
I constantly shiver in prairie sunlight.
Dark crevasses in my body, choked
by the mist of St. Petersburg nights.
Sunshine is not called for, it misses my plight.

Gold of the spire topping the Peter-Paul Fortress,
crumbling, old stairs in the Mikhailovsky park,
rain as I walk along Nevsky,
giant bronze horse on which the city rides

into the unknown
looking toward the alluring, eluding,
always-mysterious, distant West
peeking through that small window
Peter cut in the deep Russian ice.

That's where I am, in the west.
Talk to me.

My city does not give a damn,
absorbed in itself,
gazes at splendid reflections in water
not reality—
the haze of St. Petersburg nights,
shimmering pearly-white in the summer,

sun glides
not touching the ground
or the sea that lies behind.

Dusk and dawn—the identical twins of time
like hundreds of the city's bridges—
span mixed-up days and nights,
arch over the canals and rivers rushing to the delta,
spilling *toskà* into the sea,
birthing one hundred and one islands—
a memory gorge of scents and shadows to navigate
as the cold Baltic ocean overruns me.

III.
I sail the waves in my caravel.

Why a caravel?
                It's my favourite song.

The imagined and the real
live together on the deck of a ship.
I drink chocolate with Paisiello
dance a minuet in a crinoline.

Why a crinoline?
                The music I hear, the books I read.

Hazy moon looks at me
through the leaves of the weeping birch.
Snow falls.
I have new boots
go with father to visit a friend
stick out my tongue
catch the snow
as all children do.

Why snow?
                It's always with me.

The smell of melting snow—spring in Leningrad.
Where is that city?
Not on a map.
It is on an island in Nostalgia Sea
populated by me and only me.
I walk though its streets at all times of the day
touch the stones, feel twilight
peek into windows bright with my youth.
People move, people talk.
No crinoline there
just my life—
the smell of snow
the words of old songs
the sounds of music
stuck in my brain like a needle on an old record.

Why an old record?
                          That's what it is.

IV.
Serva Padrona on my TV screen,
the Rococo opera Catherine the Great enjoyed
in her private theatre at the Winter Palace
one cold snowy evening
with servants carrying refreshments
to exalted guests of the Empress
ages ago.

Why do I long
for things never seen, never felt,
chocolate pots and powdered wigs?
Or is it for my past,
for the stories told then,
my youth's melting snow,
the dirt and smell of St. Petersburg?

The palaces,
the powdered wigs,
the chocolate in the morning
have never been.

Serva Padrona,
the illusion on my TV screen
that Paisiello wrote in freezing St. Peter
for Catherine the Great
before he ran back to sunny Naples
cheating her of a year's salary
and his elegant nonsense.
Was she sad?

V.
Water swirls in the sink—
the prairies no longer an ocean
and points on the astrolabe are now
dots on the busy pages of my life
identical to one another.

Why do I sing
about watching the horizon
for over three hundred days
searching for a sign of my lost caravel?
I cannot find my coordinates
nor go back to pick up the ghosts.

Tselina

The old record player spins a new song
about two girls dancing on a small ship
sailing the Angara—
two Soviet-style romantics
building the new GES
conquering mighty rivers
plowing the virgin soil.

Song by the composer in tune
with the authorities.
My aunt and her friend discuss
who I should marry. I dance.
I already know
I don't want *tselina*.
I don't want Angara.
I do not want to marry.

I badly want that dress on top
of the old Singer to be finished for tonight.
I want to go dancing, any music will do.
This agitprop song is an old-fashioned waltz.
I spin, Angara, *tselina*, virgin.
Two seasoned women laugh at me
in the fading daylight.
There is still time.

Visit to an Ancestral Village

These are the lands we left,
choosing life over the sharp smell
of the spring-plowed fields,
this thin layer of meagre dirt of the Russian North.
Poor soil that birthed the best linen
and flax oil buried in the earth—
large clay jars of pungent amber.

These are the lands we left,
choosing life over the flowery scent
of the linden-honey,
the bees buzzing in grandpa's garden,
the lindens, the flax, the buckwheat.

The lands taken from us,
forced to be abandoned, dropped
like grandma's hand-woven linen kerchief
as she runs terrified after the last seized cow.
Gone with my mother's childhood,
her disappeared heaven.
The sea of blue flax
always hidden
behind the glint of her brown eyes.

These are my relatives.
The connections I've never suspected.
The glimmer of a hot *samovar*
on the white-clothed wooden table,
the gold of fresh-drawn honey—
the pride of the house—
spooned
from chipped, polka-dot-painted saucers.

The waft of the linden,
this aroma of loss.
The teardrops on my aunt's smiling face.
The hives? mother dreamingly asks,
could they still be...?
But the years piled up against her wild wishes,
not much is left of the past.

Only a whisper of wind in the overgrown garden,
the baffled shake of old people's heads,
the mild tang of Petersburg-style *sytnyi* bread
still baked by now-ancient Aunt Nastya,
and a shimmer of honey
hit by the light—
these multifaceted brilliants
liquefied by the centrifuge of time.

Upon Waking

an ordinary day
one of the many scattered over the plains
shattered over the rounds of time
january to january
the black hole sucking my life
second by second
into a void
as I tiptoe on the edge
forward and back
again and again

just another day to ask myself
where am I and why
another day to feel unrelated
fifth wheel on a bandwagon not mine
rolling and rolling along the prairie
no sea no canals and no fog in sight
open sky
a disconsolate horizon
fields longer than my entire life
everything so big—an overextended now
as if there will be no tomorrow

Continental Divide

I lean on different lampposts as I go
I wash my dirty laundry differently

The consonants of my language hard to pronounce
my Os are wider than yours

The place names, the people I know, tell you no more
than a Labatt's Blue twelve-pack says to me

I understand Catherine the Great better
than I comprehend my next-door neighbour

Morning Sigh

The morning's happiness is different
from the night's. Sun looks into my eyes
in search of home for the day. My coffee
puffs, a sharp wake-up. Deep golden tea
shines in your cup, my grandmother's scent,
the calming, slow-down waft. The snow
twinkles outside. Rare hoarfrost on branches
releases a torrent. Forbidden memories.
Forgotten trees. I do not talk. Drink. Eat,
ride waves of recollections hard-hitting
my safe shore. It's quiet. I hear
the earth's breath, the wind's sigh.

Black Snow

The snow of my childhood was white
for only a short time
after it fell.
Covered by black soot in a few days.
No one thought anything of it
no one talked.

Snow rolled
onto my small town
on the outskirts of St. Petersburg
like waves
and the entrance to our apartment
became sea-deep.

The only man
to navigate it
lived on the second floor.
He'd served in the navy
during the war.

He dug a system of tunnels
a maze
for ships coming to port
guided by lights from our windows
and the sour smell of *shchi*.

Bursting

Arrival
Small square in front of *Voksal*
whitewashed buildings
and crowds

Men only
their eyes cynically undressing
me

whistling, *tzoking*
I am in a miniskirt
my knees burn

Itching moves up along legs
I shake—fear, disgust
lust

Southern night falls
fast
not a taxi in sight

My panic mixes
with the intoxication of blossoming
bursts

into a dry nervous laugh
My friend waves to a man in a crowd
a neighbour

we are whisked into the night
thick with desires I want
to touch

Surrender

Sun-drenched roofs
crown
chalky-white, low houses

Golden sand melts like ice cream
into a sea's seductive
turquoise blues

Open palms of grape leaves
caress ink-purple clusters
hugged by tanned, twisted arms of aged vines

Blazing *dzhezvas* cuddle
sweeten black Turkish coffee
on the bleached, narrow streets

Heady perfume—zesty mix
of old roses, sweaty bodies
and pungent *khmeli suneli*

wraps the city—an alabaster cocoon
drifting
at leisure in the deep cerulean skies

Coffee Should Be
Black as Hell
Strong as Death
Sweet as Love

Red glowing coals in the *mangal*
On top
black metal box filled with sand

Rows of shining *dzhezvas* buried in gold grains
handles turned to face the black-mustached man
He picks one up

Scorching thick-brown-liquid-live-hell
flows into a cup
I watch every drop

My lips wet—open
ready to sip the black-strong-sweet
initiation into the mysteries of adult life

Man's vermillion mouth, white teeth
buttery eyes meet mine
I ask for more

First Fig

End of the day, half empty bazaar
Wooden planks overhead give some shade
Tired sun settles down for a night of love
Woman's eyes—old, shrewd, dark

Mound of figs
Plush purple-black
Velvet absorbing sunshine
Drops of juice in the cracks

Exploding, perfectly ripe
I bite—unexpectedly sweet, soft, lush
Fruit of Paradise
Womb—drips with seeds, excites

I am Eve
On my tongue is desire, life
Skin is bitter
I peel the next one

Overflow

Small courtyard
overwhelmed by the midday sun
low, laden table and bench
meltingly warm

Isabella aged
into thick, voluptuous
sensuous nectar
flows into my glass

Drops of vine's blood
spill
on a white polished stone
I bend

Heady scent hits my nostrils
hints of hot bodies
Pink tongue out
I lip inky liquor   cat style

Dripping

Narrow shortcut
between
whitewashed walls

punctuated
by entwined green limbs
of heavy vine

Dark purple clusters
ripened breasts, laden, erupting
Buzzing sound—

flies
gorge in the splits
break the stillness of noon air

My beach bag
stuffed full, I crush into the wall
squeeze nipple after nipple

Violet-red *Isabella*'s juice
warm
drips along my naked thigh

Laden Sated Weighted

I melt into a golden sand
warm and yielding
under my languorous limbs
under my flooded breasts

My head turns
to the boy beside me
I am drowsy
inhale sun-stirred-man-heat

palpable
tingling
penetrating
all the way down

Turkish Bath Is Century Old

Old woman
hair still jet black
dry skin hangs on bones
lets us in

Grey marble
softened
by moist women's thighs
brushing wet walls

Seats glisten
polished
by women's buttocks
steamy and lush

Three young girls
breasts sway
hips swing
naked skin bursts from heat
like the overripe fig at the bazaar

I pour hot water
from a shiny aluminum tub
on my slippery
lathered body

White suds
slide
along my saturated limbs

Appetite

Outdoor oven
grey stone
like a fairy tale giant
red burning mouth into which
khachapuri is thrown

Lustful eyes follow each one
in and out
jealous of the diners
who bite and chew
mouthfuls of dripping hot *suluguni*
enclosed
in a blackened yeast-smelling crust

as the setting sun welcomes
starry, stuffy southern night

Fortune-Telling

When the city dons her silk gown of night
holes punched for gazing stars
and crawls to the shore
an odalisque to be touched
by spindrift at the crest of the waves

an old Greek woman born from the dark
emerges in our kitchen light
Seductress
with sparkling tales of a future
for each one of us

Her wrinkled fingers
swollen at knuckles
a long mixing spoon
round and round at the bottom of *dzhezva*
calling all demons to come

I gulp the bittersweet heat of my life
bottom up, hand her an empty cup
to conjure love
from the intricate patterns
of brownish foam and coffee slush

Night

At night the sea comes to visit
drapes the city
in a thick voluptuous mist
oozing seashell whispers
among
the twisting
        curving
                searching
                        burning
lips
legs
breasts

Hot sweat drips on damp sheets

Shrivelling

In the morning women hang
wet bedding on white clotheslines
stretched across narrow yards

Night's longings sway in the breeze
as I lie alone on the roof
sun kissing my naked breasts

Sweet smell of overripe, oozing grapes
heady as they shrivel into raisins
on a hot metal tray

Do You Remember Our Life?

Piano sounds sparkling in crystal lights
in the white philharmonic hall, we—above
Rustle of leaves under our feet
in the marble of autumn with gods in a park
Yellow glimmer of water droplets
in the mist of dark Petergof, on a bench
Sounds of trams
crowds in the metro
bridges raised in the middle of night

Can you remember?
Saint-Saëns concerto in a room full of love
sound of a spoon on the bottom of a *dzhezva*
turn of the key at the entrance door
Cries of our daughter at night
taste of black tea
nicked pink rose cup
Cold Baltic winds over the city
watery reflections in our eyes

Wetness of streets grey from the rain
Black railings of bridges white from the frost
Granite embankments and palaces' lights
Ice on the Neva
lilacs in bloom
melting of snow in St. Petersburg

Dust on dry hellebores in a jar
fragrance of soup in a pot on the stove
Mornings a parting to last through the day
Echoes of kisses
warmth of embraces
Sound of our bodies at night
Do you remember our life?

On His Breath

As long as this man holds on to his life,
breathes through a respirator
in and out,
in a measured way,
I still have the earthy odour of the *podval*
he dug out under the floor in the hallway.

Tall glass jars line the shelves of dirt
dressed in thin strips of pine board.
My aunt's inky bounty of black currant jam
vies with the pinky blush
of southern-vacation-peaches
and a lucky purchase of Polish dill pickles.

I can still cross
the bridge over the narrow stream
we all called "shitty-river"
and speed down the hill
onto the ice-shielded Neva
in my beaten, old wooden sled.

I can skate
on the snow-packed streets,
pick mushrooms
among awakening aspens.
Grass still wet from the morning's dew
as my mother's voice searches for me—"ah-oo."

Cabbage pie waits for me on the scrubbed kitchen table.
Butter melts on pie crust,
mother's face glistens
from happiness and sweat as we drink
strong hot tea steeped in a small, white teapot,
rose blooms on its fat, crackled cheek.

I can still taste
my first sip of *Soviet Champagne*.
Dark-green bottle.
Its silver-wrapped throat
graces the table laden with my mother's jellied beef,
Olivier salad, and herring-under-the-fur-coat,

reflects
the golden threads of the New Year tree
and the silver TV screen
where young Kosmonauts dance
with an even younger
Soviet singer Larisa Mondrus.

I can move any time
in and out
of my small town on the outskirts of Leningrad.
I need no ticket,
no passport to cross the formidable border
into my childhood,
in and out.

As long as my father holds on.

Night Vigil

Dreams interrupted,
snippets of conversation,
memories, headache, indigestion,
images of the past, faces, bridges,
the smell of snow.

Counting sheep, sleep, wake up, sleep.
Mother's voice, attack of nostalgia,
muscle cramp, deep sighs,
torture,
ordeal.

Pierced on the spit of night,
I turn and turn,
roast under the slow fire
of guilt, regret,
morning's dread.

In the Family Room

Many shadows live in this room,
hide on shelves between the pages of books.
Words fly
like dust motes in a filtered sun,
shift
as hot air from the register moves the grey blind.

I doze on the old couch,
snow melts in my sleep,
a river floods hopes, desires, and dreams.
Cookbooks and movies swirl as they pass,
raft with the operas,
boats with roasts.

An old eucalyptus lands
in the middle of a bridge—
the marble Rialto where I, motionless, stand,
forty-year-old cake in my hands,
mummified in my memory
with my mother's vanilla smell.

Voices and voices,
languages mix,
Russian of Pushkin, English from Austin,
Gumilev and Akhmatova together again.
Mandelshtam lives,
Brodsky ardently argues with him.

Photographs, pages with party notes, recipes,
dinner-guest lists, and poems
fold into paper airplanes and take off,
jet into coming twilight,
saved from the drowning
as the years form into a waterfall

and come crashing,
carry life's trinkets with them,
foam and scum
as the water hits bottom.
Mayday branches and lilac blossoms
float on top,

washed ashore
at a small island of memories,
there is another,
one more and one more,
one hundred and one—crowded archipelago
populated by people I love.

Their voices echo inside me
languages mixed,
words fly,
shadows pass,
as I spread my hands like a net—
try to catch and hold each one.

Sea Waves

I had a dream in colour—teal—the undulating waves of it.
Lapels on mother's jacket—embroidery—
and all the fuss, connections, efforts.

The atelier on Nevsky, where the manager
greeted us with pomp and circumstance.
We were the chosen ones.

The seamstress hovered above my mother,
tape measure in her hands
flew up and down,

and then they asked about colour.
My mother held her breath and said,
the sea-wave, please

and everybody paused.
I thought how daring—
to aspire to the height of the Soviet colour-pantheon.

We waited, not too long—
my father's lumber promise opened so many doors.
The stocky woman nodded,

there will be no problems,
asked mother to come for a fitting
in two weeks, but pay deposit now.

The suit materialized a month later.
The dark sea-wave hugged my mother many years
and now colours my nights.

Roman Bus

Somehow I am still on the bus
turning from via Nazionale
to del Corso in the fading December

daylight. Behind—the white pomposity
of Vittorio Emmanuelle's monument.
Vast proportions of its Victorian swags

cripple the nation's celebratory cake.
In a small niche of the first building,
as the bus straightens along the street,

small crèche: baby Jesus, light over
his crib, Josef and Mary behind,
animals, shepherds, magi. My repeated

surprise, the foreignness of the sight
removed from my life. My daughter's
pointed finger. Who is that baby, why?

The winter without the snow,
the newness of the world born to us.
I am on that bus, on that bus.

Two Knit, Two Purl

Musty whiff of old wool.
This sweater lived in a suitcase
for twenty years.

Its marsh colour now in unison
with its scent—dusty, mouldy
green, spots of white paint.

My father was the last one
to wear it when he came to visit
and painted the fence one cold autumn day.

I had knitted the sweater for my husband.
By that time
he had worn it long enough.

The stale odour fills the room as I sit
with my knitting needles, unused for two
decades, and a ball of thirty-year-old wool.

I count stitches—two purl, two knit,
ten purl, two knit, trying to find the key...
knit a blanket for my granddaughter.

Double-Edged

Yesterday at noon
as Brodsky's verses triggered a response
my poem gushed forth—in Russian
fast, a surging river in the spring, smashed
uneven layers of a carefully constructed dam
and I have lost my hidden battle with the past

The words—the melody inborn
each one understood and felt
like friends in sweat-inducing dreams
that I am scared to remember
Forgotten intonation frightened me
I do not want to return there

But how sweet the ease
with which the sounds dance
the ballet on the old Mariinsky stage
light, gracious, all white, seductive
the Mayday flowers I want to shake from branches
quash gauzy petals at my weary feet

Rupture

Autumn arrives
leisurely, tentative steps
one at a time, no rush.

As if she knows
I am reluctant to part with summer
grants me more time.

This most empathic season of year
honours the last sighs
of the dying leaves

paints pale sky
in a symphony of blues and greys
carefully choosing her shades.

Days fall faster, softer
lose the brilliance of bright sun.
Age's patina spreads on the shivering grass.

Autumn gently strokes the yearning ground.
Frosty marks of her fingers—
a reminder of passing time.

High in the sky, flocks of birds
fly together.
Nobody is left behind.

Almost a Recipe

My mother's signature dish—*golubtsi*
—cabbage rolls—
a Sunday ritual performed on the only day off

She starts pulling large outer leaves from the cabbage
drops them into the pot of boiling water to blanch
My father pushes the meat through the grinder

as I am just waking up
My breakfast waits on the table's corner
my brother locked in his room, some Western music pumping

She mixes the filling—meat, onions, and rice
Mother and I shape the rolls together
set them on the warped wooden board

Father adds more logs to heat up the stove
She is ready to blast—
fries each piece on a skillet until brown

places them into a tomato-sauce-filled *utatnitza*
(Duck Pot—so-called from the pre-Revolutionary days
when ducks were around and deserved their own pot)

No cans to open, she makes everything from scratch
fills the pot to the brink—browned rolls, tomato sauce
lots of pepper and salt, and pieces of onion tucked in

The pot in the oven—she has some time for a cup of tea
and the clean up
Our kitchen is small, only one table for all

The aroma now coming from the oven is so enticing
we can't leave the house
gather around the fridge checking the supply of sour cream

Two hours later the *golubtsi* are ready
The blue-rimed plates on the table
mother serves us—

hot orange rolls in a pool of the red tomato sauce
with the huge dollops of white sour cream
—cold

Queen of the Neva

Early spring. Sun melts snow banks
and moon freezes them.
The celestial couple's mischievous fling
on the river shore
erects shimmering icy palaces—
a fairy tale town for me to explore.

Alone
I stand in the slush and dream,
pick up pieces of frozen Scheherazade's city
building by building,
street by street.

Sun plays lightheartedly on the intricate walls
that sparkle and sing under its rays.
Each icicle serenades—
crystal clear, capricious beauty
at every turn.

A symphony of glimmer—
enchanted, effervescent realm
where I am the queen—
reverie in my fantasy
forgetting the time of the day.

Each twist of frosty gothic spire
flickers into a glittering tale.
I compose the magical stories
about this bewitched kingdom
vanishing in front of my eyes

until my toes hurt from cold.
I realize—my boots are wet,
my frozen throne is thawing,
my coat is heavy with icy water.
I run home as fast as I can.

Volodia

In the sixties when Khrushchev decided
to catch up and overtake America
we were all lining up for bread—
those of us lucky enough
to live in the big cities where bread
was still available.
Everybody else ate
some of the dreamed-up corn
that he had commanded us
to plant everywhere
thinking about prosperity.
We got semi-starvation instead.

At the same time we were the first ones
to send a man into the *cosmos*
to check whether God was there.
Don't laugh.
It became the favourite argument—
Gagarin was there
and he did not see God.
Funny, as if God could be seen.
But the Soviets liked straight answers
and marching in overwhelming numbers.

I went to school during those times.
Put on the uniform, a brown wool dress
and white silk apron made by my aunt.
I was a tomboy.

The teachers often called my mother to school.
I started a fight, beat a boy—
my upstairs neighbour
or another one I really liked.
Blue eyes, blond hair—my total opposite.
He and his mother just moved from Leningrad
to our small town on the outskirts.
He sure was putting on airs—had to be beaten.
How else to deal
with an unearned sense of superiority?

This kid, Volodia, was pretty smart.
When he figured out
he could not boss me around
we became friends.
I went to his home to read books and drink tea.
I made sure I got better marks than he.
Without warning, they moved out
over the summer.
We did not say goodbye.
It was not such a big deal then.
But I would like to see his photograph now—
burned with all my childhood memorabilia
when I left.
All I remember,
his eyes were so blue.

That One Small Step

Forty years after the event
I watch man land on the moon
on my new big-screen TV

The whole earth watched
that moment
but we in the Soviet Union
did not know
did not see

We were not part of the whole
we were a different tribe
not earthlings

As We Trot the Surface of the Globe

Almodrote

The Sounds

Spain is a country of shadows and ghosts.
It's your choice to see them or not.
But how can you not hear them?
Their voices echo your steps as you walk
along narrow streets of Santa Cruz in Seville.

Their sighs fill the courtyards of old Jewish towns,
Moorish fortresses, and every port
from where they had to leave,
crowding into the tiny boats
sailing into unknown.

On a small Maimonides Square
shadows argue fine points of Talmud.
Ghosts sing Flamenco,
glottal voices bounce among barren Andalusia's hills.
Their prayers hang heavy in the air of a Cordova mosque.

Time holds no meaning in the face of such sorrows.
Just listen.
In Granada's Cathedral, the past crowds
around Isabella's tomb,
asks the same age-old question.

Why?

The Switch

How long does it take to forget one country
and create a new one in its place?

How long to invent Spanish tortilla with potatoes
from the New World and forbid an *almodrote*?

How long is the walk from alcázar to fortress,
from mosque to cathedral, from synagogue to church?

Is it a few minutes along the streets of Seville
or centuries of pain?

New being is born from the obliterated old.
Could anything have been different?

At the Arch of Titus

1.
I was not in Rome when Titus came back
from the campaign in Judea. I did not walk
under his triumphal arch, and no other Jew
walked under it for two thousand years.

Victory over a rebellious nation,
a small country daring to defy mighty Rome,
daring to fight for freedom.
Four legions, four years of war.

Brutal siege of Jerusalem,
hundreds of thousands dead in famine.
Final assault. Walls breached. Temple burned.
The loot, the sacred vessels carried to Rome,

menorah on the Arch of Titus,
the crux of our history, source of our suffering.
Jerusalem lost. We are dispersed.
Vespasian's proudly minted coins, "Judaea Capta."

We wander for two thousand years,
carry the light of the temple in our hearts,
the name of Jerusalem on our lips.
I look at the arch,

imposing, among ruins of Roman Forum,
as if God kept it for a purpose.
I can't touch it. I can't walk under it,
an ancient monument guarded by metal railing.

Hot sun above. Dust of time under my feet.
Sharp smell of Roman pines, birds cross clear blue sky.
I am just one among millions of tourists
gazing at the remains of Imperial Rome.

2.
There is the monument to our fall—
Arch of Titus on the hills of the Roman Forum.
Menorah on the side, Jewish prisoners led into captivity.

End of Judea.

There is the monument to our suffering—
Arch of Constantine on the hills of the Roman Forum.
Christianity proclaimed as the religion of the Empire.

Dawn of our persecution.

Arches stand next to each other
among the ruins of Roman Empire.
Where is the arch to our survival?

1492

1492—four-digit number,
behind—faces, voices, tears, cries.
Turning points. The end and beginning.

1492—a line on a piece of a paper,
behind—boats at sea. Empty-eyed refugees
disembark on unwelcoming shores.

1492—wailing on squares as crosses are carried
over bent heads. Silence and whispers
as ancient prayers leave the lips of the old.

1492—parents die among their Christian
daughters and sons, hush, hush, hush, shush,
shush, shush, forget who we are.

1492—abandoned towns, scorched fields, earth
smouldering under exiles' feet, inquisition's black
hoods, market squares smelling of burned human flesh.

El Transito Synagogue

I carry with me a guidebook
about a big synagogue in Toledo.
The place was rife with life a long time ago,
now an empty shell, desolate.

Echoes bounce off bare, grey stone walls.
On the columns—carved scrolls
of pomegranate trees
faded under the centuries of hiding.

We can only imagine
women in rich mantillas crowding the balconies
under Lebanon's cedar ceiling
laughing, gossiping against rabbi's laws.

Indifferent tourists look at sparse exhibits,
remnants—stripped of any life.
The streets around so narrow,
we touch opposite dwellings spreading our arms.

We do not know how people lived.
Were they happy? Did they dance?
We only know they were expelled.
Had to go. Had to leave their homes.

The lands, the buildings,
and the ones buried in the cemeteries
could not be moved.
Were left behind.

Toledo Bookstore

A lonely bookstore, *Sephardim* inside.
They've come back here
to live in the city of their ancestors
five hundred years later.

We buy a book, *Sephardic History*.
This shop is so full of melancholy
I am ready to wail. We make our way
back to the hotel in a throng of tourists.

The city's carnival starts tonight.
You stop, suddenly, say, *we need to return.*
We have the wrong book.
It is the Ladino Dictionary.

Young man at the store has mixed up
the history of his people with desire
to say in his own language
the story of this city as he remembers it.

We rush back.
The shop is closed.
There is Jewish Sabbath in the city of Toledo
in this year of our Lord.

Giudecca Street

I stand at the corner
look to the back and front
search on the left and right
peer diagonally.

Not a trace of our presence
nor sound of our voices
no smell of our food
no *almodrote*.

Above my head
a street name on the plaque

Giudecca—desperate screams
from gagged mouths
among grey, crumbling stones
silent for centuries.

Cordova

I buy a scarf
orange and yellow, a golden fringe.
I find it in one of the stalls
crowding little square

we pass by on our way
along the wide boulevard
lined with blossoming orange trees
heading to old quarter of Cordova

to look at the little courtyards
on the twisted, narrow, white-washed streets
empty of its Jewish inhabitants
long time ago.

I know.
I know.
The wrong scarf.
It should be black.

Our Faces

On the wall of the Prado
in a heavy gold frame
I see a four-hundred-year-old portrait
of my cousin Garik
painted by El Greco
hundred years after we fled from Spain.

On my finger I wear a gold ring
with two hands joined together
over the small box hiding the *ketubah*.
Stars and crescent moons on its sides.
The year—1492—engraved
to remember.

You bought the ring for me in a small store
in Toledo, not far from El Greco's house
that used to be a Synagogue
hundred years before he came from Greece
and painted
the faces of *conversos* who stayed behind

as if they are Christian Saints—dramatic lines,
expressive eyes, tortured souls, and nightmares for memories.
These are El Greco's best portraits—
black-haired, Jewish-eyed Spaniards.
My long-lost cousins
walking the streets of Madrid.

Cooking Almodrote

I chop grilled eggplant in my kitchen in Canada,
mix it with eggs, grate some hard cheese.
I am cooking a dish
common in Spain before the expulsion
in 1492.
I make *almodrote*.
Nobody knocks on my door,
drags me to the Inquisition's death chambers
for cooking a favourite meal
or washing on Friday,
sure signs of the heretic to be tortured and burned.
Every citizen had to convert
in the reborn Catholic Spain,
had to pray to a different god,
sing the new songs,
change their names and their voices
and to forget the cherished *almodrote*.

How far is it from that Spain to Soviet Russia?

Every citizen had to swallow the new religion,
sing the communist's song,
march to the victory music,
or be killed
for reading a forbidden book,
getting a letter from a sister or a friend
who had the luck to escape,
for saying or even thinking unapproved thoughts.
No fires were burning—
different times—different methods.
Guns. Hunger. Frost. Forced labour.
One had to bend. One had to submit.

I better attend to my *almodrote*.
Looks like I grated too much cheese.
These old dishes are used to travelling.
We add new ingredients
as we trot the surface of the globe.
I now put cellophane noodles into my *kulebiaka*.
Makes a fine substitute for something I left behind.

White Petals

1.
What I dream is not here
I hear sounds, voices gone long ago

Boabdil's last sigh, leaves' rustle
White gravel path, rose petals blown by the wind

Bright ranunculus open
Water drops, smell of mirth

Me, my bed, worn-out book
Mirage of the garden I will never see

Outside, my mother's sweet-smelling
Mock-orange-jasmine

In this Russian North snow falls
White petals behind Boabdil

2.
Rahel la Fermosa—the beautiful. Black-haired
Bright-eyed Jewish girl, King Alfonso's beloved

Her dead body, stabbed. His silent tears drop
On the marble floor of the Moorish palace

Arabic scrolls on tiled walls, pink and white roses
Gaze into the still waters of garden pools

Small boy, their son, a white gravel path leads him away
I am fifteen, I cry, mix palaces in my dreams

My ghosts live in green hills of Toledo
Years later I am going to Alhambra alone

3.
The road to Alhambra lined with roses
Pink and white petals tremble

White cloud in front of the palace
Six bushes, clipped, coiffed. Leaves rustle

Sweet-smelling mock-orange-jasmine
The link to my North by Boabdil

4.
Sun heats the rows of clipped cedars
Raises a sharp resinous smell into hot air

Whispers lift from thick needles
Lovers words interrupted fall unfinished

On the beige shale of the grounds
Drops of blood like ranunculus opened up

5.
Myrtle pool, waters of paradise
Still, heavy with tears of Boabdil

Courtyard of Lions, fountain
White stone, carved

Twelve lions, twelve Zodiac signs
Embody eternity, entirety of time

Water stops flowing, lions' jaws dry
When Queen Isabella rides in

Time stops.

6.
Now rain drips on Alhambra
Metamorphoses into snow

White flakes melt upon tiled walls
Faded blue, red, turquoise

Snow whispering into my ear
Harem's chorus, tambourine sounds

Light, airy stone, snow falls through
On the fountain below

Moorish arches, garden sleeps
Waters still, grey like this winter day

Snowflakes—white petals
Cover the gaping mouth of Boabdil

7.
I am chilled. To the bone. Snow falls
White on black—sharp contrast

Black and white—dream and waking up
Past and present, a divide

I retreat to a bookstore. Alhambra on the page
Maps, dates, names of Sultans, reigns

No more whisper. Heavy book
Knowledge weighs on my mind

8.
Noisy, narrow, crooked streets of Albayzín
Bright trinkets inside tiny stores

Glow like Gypsy's eyes in the heat of the night
Hand-painted fans, clothing, mix of Morocco and Spain

English sounds in crowded restaurants
I do not enter, only inhale

Make my way through the rowdy labyrinth
Above, on the hill, among cypresses green

Imposing, red brick walls of Alhambra
Regal in their final, lasting defeat

I find a silver tea strainer in a pile of old junk
A practical object to buy

Out of place in this cheap, clattery Gypsy bazaar
Just like carved windows, diaphanous veils

Sweet smell of roses, blood in the fountain, soft whispers
Gold slippers, Boabdil's tears, white petals, and I

9.
I do not dream anymore of Alhambra
Dreams, once touched   disappear

I do not hear Fermosa or see Boabdil
We have parted. I look at the pictures in the thick book

Printed tiles blue, red, turquoise
Still images of garden pools

In this northern land wind blows
White petals from my mock-orange-jasmine

~

Notes on the Poems

"Variations on Twilight"
Symerki—Russian for twilight, the time after a sunset before darkness of night

"Chalat"
Chalat—Russian for housecoat

"Sunday Morning Breakfast"
Tabor—Gypsy camp

Shalvar—Traditional Turkish baggy trousers

Tanbur—Traditional long-necked string instrument used in Turkey

"Solaris"
Solaris—1972 sci-fi movie by Russian director Andrei Tarkovsky. Tarkovsky's groundbreaking psychological drama was based on Stanislaw Lem's 1961 novel of the same name.

"Reading Brodsky"
Rukav—Russian for sleeve

Toskà—inexplicable, indefinite feeling which hints at unappeasable heartache, insatiate longing

"A Vast Sea"
The Scarlet Sails is a festival in St. Petersburg to celebrate school graduation, usually on the longest day of the year. The peak of the celebration is the floating of a boat with raised scarlet sails along the Neva. The Scarlet Sails symbolize the possibility of a dream becoming a reality and is based on a very popular 1923 romantic novel by Alexander Grin.

Peter the First founded St. Petersburg in 1703. It was the first Russian seaport through which Russia could trade with the West and so became "the window" to the West. In the words of A. Pushkin, "Here the fate decided/we will cut window to Europe/Firmly put our feet onto sea."

The city was founded at the delta of the river Neva which in XVIII century had forty-eight rivers and canals and one hundred and one islands.

"Tselina"
Tselina—Virgin Lands; also slang for virgin

"Visit to an Ancentral Village"
Sytnyi—Bread baked from a finely ground flour usually available in a city, not in a village

"Black Snow"
Schti—Russian sauerkraut soup

"Bursting"
Voksal—train station

Tzoking—making short TZ sounds of appreciation

Dzhezva—a metal pot with one handle in which to make Turkish coffee

Khmeli suneli—Georgian spice mix widely used in Caucasus

Mangal—Turkish barbeque

Isabella—variety of grape grown in Abkhazia

Khachapuri—traditional Georgian pie baked on the open flames

Suluguni—traditional Georgian cheese

"Do You Remember Our Life"
Dzhezva—a metal pot with one handle in which to make Turkish coffee

"On His Breath"
Podval—Russian for cellar

As We Trot the Surface of the Globe
These poems were written during my travels through Spain. Three major religions coexisted in Spain during Mediaeval times. This coexistence ended in 1492 with the fall of the last Moorish kingdom of Granada and the expulsion of Jews.

"Almodrote"
Almodrote—Spanish Jewish dish, predates 1492. Almodrote is an

omelette-like dish made from eggplant, cheese, and eggs. It can be fried on a skillet and flipped to cook both sides or baked in an oven.

Sephardim—the descendants of Jews who left Spain and Portugal after the 1492 expulsion

Ladino—the language of Spanish Jews

Giudecca—corruption of the Latin *Judaica*, maybe translated as Jewish

Ketuba—traditional Jewish marriage contract

Kulebiaka—traditional Russian fish pie. Cellophane noodles substitute Vesiga, which is dry sturgeon marrow that provides the gelatinous texture in Kulebiaka.

"White Petals"
Boabdil—the last Moorish king of Alhambra in Granada, Spain

Queen Isabella—Isabella I of Castile

Acknowledgements

The poems "Two Knit, Two Purl" (different format), "God Came down for Beauty," and "We Expected Sedona to Be Red and Warm" were published in annual issues of *Stroll of Poets Anthology*, published by Edmonton Stroll of Poets Society. The poems "Air" and "Morning Sigh" (under the title "Simmer") were published in *Sun and Snow Anthology*, published by Rhythm International Foundation of Edmonton.

I am grateful to Alice Major and Pierrette Requier for their continuous encouragement and support.

Thank you to the members of the "Living Room" poets—the first listeners of many poems in this book—for their welcome and friendship.

Heartfelt thanks to Sharon Caseburg for her insights into my poetry and inspiration to chisel each poem to the best it could be. Thank you to Sarah Ens for an expert proofreading and to Jamis Paulson for the book cover that catches the spirit of my poetry.